S/HE

Titles in the series:

DELETE
TIM COLLINS

IN THE STARS
ECHO FREER

KEEPER
ANN EVANS

KILL ORDER
DANIEL BLYTHE

LAST YEAR
IAIN McLAUGHLIN

PARADISE
TIM COLLINS

S/HE
CATHERINE BRUTON

THE CRAVING
CLIFF McNISH

Badger Publishing Limited, Oldmedow Road, Hardwick Industrial Estate,
King's Lynn PE30 4JJ

Telephone: 01438 791037

www.badgerlearning.co.uk

S/HE

CATHERINE BRUTON

S/HE ISBN 978-1-78464-698-1

Publisher: Susan Ross
Senior Editor: Danny Pearson
Copyediting: Cambridge Publishing Management Ltd
Designer: Bigtop Design Ltd
Cover: Trigger Image / Alamy

2 4 6 8 10 9 7 5 3 1

CHAPTER 1
RAVEN

When the new kid walked into maths on Wednesday morning, Kat woke up. Fast.

Tall, slender, with broad shoulders, shoulder-length black hair, piercing blue eyes and a face that was kind of beautiful in a boyish sort of way, the new kid made *everyone* wake up. Even Queen Bee Saskia stopped texting and whispered loudly, 'Check out the new talent, ladies!'

Mr Moles was less impressed.

'Young man, you are wearing make-up!'

'Actually, I'm not....'

'I can see lipstick,' Mr Moles insisted. 'And… is that blusher on your cheeks, boy?'

'Yes, sir,' the new kid replied. 'But I'm not a boy.'

'Don't answer me back, young man.'

'I'm not a young man, either.'

Mr Moles stared at the new kid, his eyelid twitching nervously.

'This should be interesting,' Saskia whispered.

'Are you trying to tell me you're a *girl*?' Mr Moles enquired, looking perplexed and rather flustered. 'Because you're wearing boys' uniform, I see.'

'No,' the new kid answered evenly. 'I'm saying I'm not a boy *or* a girl.'

'What the….' Jammo sat at the very back of the classroom, his lip curling in disgust.

His mate Gollum gurgled like an oversized baby. 'How's that then?'

'It's all in my school records, sir,' the new kid explained politely. 'I'm "gender-fluid". Some days I feel more like a boy, other days more like a girl.'

'Whoa!' said Saskia. 'I like it!'

Mr Moles just looked irritated now. 'Yes, I seem to recall the headmaster mentioning something in briefing....' He glanced down at the names in his register. 'You must be....'

'Raven,' said the new kid.

'What kind of a name is Raven?' scoffed Jammo.

'A sexy one.' Saskia shot the new kid one of her famous 'you-know-you-can't-resist-me' looks. Raven ignored it, blue eyes catching Kat's brown ones – just for a second – across the classroom.

'OK, OK, everyone settle down,' Mr Moles muttered crossly. 'Well – um – Raven, I'm afraid school uniform rules still apply.'

‘But I’ve read the school rules,’ said Raven, winking at Kat then turning back to Mr Moles, all politeness. ‘Girls can wear a small amount of make up so long as it’s discreet.’

‘But you said you’re not….’

‘And since I’m not a boy, the “hair above the shoulder” rule doesn’t apply either,’ Raven continued. ‘Now, may I sit down, sir?’

Mr Moles opened his mouth but was unable to come up with a reply. Raven slid into a chair on the front row, blue eyes twinkling. Saskia giggled, Gollum snickered – even Jammo snorted.

Things were *not* going to be boring with the new kid in town.

CHAPTER 2

MIXED DOUBLES?

Kat had always been the invisible girl. Teachers forgot her name, other students knew her as 'the quiet one' who hung out with Saskia's gang. She seemed to go through school without really ever being noticed by anyone.

Raven made heads turn from the moment of stepping into a room. There was *nothing* invisible about Raven.

And the one question on everyone's mind was the one question Raven refused to answer.

In English, Miss Daniels divided the class into boys and girls.

'Where's Raven gonna go, Miss?' asked Jammo.

'Raven? Oh, yes….' Miss Daniels looked confused for a moment. 'Well – um – where would you like to go, Raven?'

Raven shrugged, lip slightly curved into a smile. 'I'll go with the boys today, Miss. Thanks for asking.'

'OK, boys and girls….' Miss Daniels started to say, then she glanced at Raven and went slightly pink. 'I mean… students, for homework I want you to pair up – boy/girl – to do a presentation on your favourite books.'

'Raven, you can work with me,' Saskia piped up.

Saskia Hardcastle was all long legs, long blonde hair and long sharp fingernails. Since Year 7, no boy – or girl – had ever been able to resist her charms.

But Raven – apparently – was neither. Or both. Either way, Saskia's magic wasn't working.

'No, thanks. I've already got a partner.'

As Saskia's face puckered to a frown, Kat realised Raven was looking at her.

'That is – if you want to, Kat?'

The new kid knew her name! Kat couldn't quite believe it.

'Sure – I mean, yeah.'

'A Raven and a Cat. Sounds like a good team to me,' said Raven.

'Yeah but is it girl-on-girl action,' said Jammo, 'Or mixed doubles?'

'Now that,' said Raven with a shrug, 'would be telling.'

CHAPTER 3

ORLANDO

The rest of the morning's lessons were much the same. Most of the teachers had been briefed on Raven's boy/girl status. Some were better at handling it than others.

'Hey, new kid,' said Mr Lilley in PE 'Do you want to play rugby or hockey? Your choice.'

'I was pretty good at hockey at my old school,' said Raven.

'Well, that doesn't tell us anything,' Saskia whispered loudly. 'Boys and girls both play hockey.'

'Girls can play rugby too,' said Mr Lilley.

'Yeah but Raven is far too beautiful to be a rugby player,' Saskia said, glancing at Jammo – who was the school's rugby captain – and smirking.

It turned out Raven was a superb player: lithe, fast, and deft with the ball.

'What is wrong with you girls today?' Mr Lilley yelled at half-time. 'None of you are concentrating on the game.'

Raven was the problem, of course. Half of the class was entranced by this gorgeous creature. The other half was jealous. Everyone wanted to know more.

*

At lunchtime, Kat stopped being invisible. It started when Raven walked across the dining room and sank down in the seat next to hers.

'So, book buddy,' she heard herself being asked, 'what's your fave book then?'

Kat felt herself colouring. It felt like everyone in the whole dining hall was watching her. Saskia was scowling crossly at her from across the table.

She tried to act normal. 'Um – I guess – *Orlando* by Virginia Woolf'

Raven's face broke into a smile. 'Seriously? I *love* that book.'

'OK, what's this *a-mazing* book about then?' demanded Saskia loudly.

'Well. The main character, Orlando, is sort of a time traveller,' Kat explained.

'Like Doctor Who?' Saskia giggled.

'Kind of – I guess – only he… well she… keeps coming back in different bodies.'

'Like Voldemort! Or Hannah Montana?'

'Not exactly.' Kat felt herself colouring hotly. 'Orlando is sometimes a girl, sometimes a boy.'

'Sounds irresistible!' Saskia's eyes fixed on Raven now. 'So, does this Orlando fancy boys or girls?'

The question fell off her lips and hung in the air for a moment before Raven answered.

'Both, I guess.'

'I see,' said Saskia, her eyes tracing over Raven's face, the hint of eyeliner around the blue eyes, then sliding down over the long, sensitive fingers – nails painted a subtle shade of coral. 'So if you're – what did you call it – transgender?'

'Gender-fluid,' said Raven.

'Right – so if you're gender-fluid it means you're also bisexual then?'

'Not necessarily,' said Raven, patiently. 'Every gender-fluid person is different. Personally, I just fancy girls.'

'Good to know,' said Saskia with her trademark pout. 'I'll keep that in mind!'

CHAPTER 4

NEUTER NOUNS

Things got more complicated the next morning when Raven turned up in girls' uniform, hair pulled back in a ponytail, no make-up and looking sexier than ever. Kat didn't know how to feel – or where to look. And Raven kept looking at her, which made things worse… or better… she wasn't even sure she knew which any more.

In German they were studying noun classes. 'Many languages such as German and Russian have masculine, feminine and neuter nouns,' explained Mr Sillerton, his voice a sleep-inducing monotone. 'Typically, this is based on the natural gender of the referent, so male nouns are masculine, female nouns are feminine and nouns denoting some sexless objects are neuter.'

'Neuter – ha!' laughed Jammo. 'You hear that Raven? Sexless!'

'Sir?' said Raven, ignoring Jammo. 'Neuter can also mean neutral, right? Not sexless but both sexes.'

'Yes, in some instances....'

'Doubly sexy,' said Saskia.

'Sexy – a boy in a skirt!' scoffed Gollum.

'Girls like someone who's manly but in touch with their feminine side,' said Saskia, trying – unsuccessfully – to catch Raven's eye. 'You should try it some time.'

*

'So, I could come over to yours tonight and work on the project.'

Kat looked up. It was afternoon registration. Raven had just slid into the seat next to hers and was looking at her with those intensely blue eyes.

'Yeah – that would be… great!'

'Great!'

'Super-doo!' Saskia simpered sarcastically.

Mr Moles was taking the register that afternoon and he was looking flustered, as usual. Saskia's hand shot up in the air.

'Mr Moles, sir,' she said in her best star student voice. 'Can I ask you something a bit delicate?'

'Yes, Miss Hardcastle.'

'The thing is, Raven has been using the girls' toilets.'

Mr Moles glanced at Raven who did not meet his eye.

Kat had been doing her research. She knew that although the school had agreed to respect Raven's gender-fluid identity, all students had to record their legal status. On the register, Raven would be marked as a boy or girl, for all the teachers to see.

'I see.' Mr Moles shifted uncomfortably.

'And, some of the girls just don't feel completely comfortable about it. Cos Raven isn't a girl, right?'

Raven glanced up at Mr Moles nervously.

'I believe the headmaster is looking into – um – alternative arrangements,' Mr Moles stuttered, blinking a little too rapidly. 'Until then... I suppose... Raven, well, can you use the boys' toilets?'

'Whoa – we don't want the gender bender in with us!' said Jammo.

'And I don't want... ' Raven started to protest.

'It's only for a couple of days,' said Mr Moles. 'Until then, we all need to be…' he paused and blinked several times, 'flexible.'

CHAPTER 5
BITS

'Look, mate, quit messing around!'

'I'm not your mate and I'm not messing. People have a right to know.'

'To know what?' Raven stood outside the boys' toilets, squaring up to a leering Jammo and a bunch of his mates.

'If you're Arthur or Martha!' Jammo's face was scrunched up like a fist.

'Yeah, we gotta know if you've got a dick or a fanny,' added Gollum bluntly.

'What about my right to privacy?' Raven demanded, eyes flashing dangerously. 'I go to the loo and you and your cronies start climbing over the stall, sticking your heads under the door. That's OK, how?'

'Freedom of information, innit,' said Jammo. 'Peeps wanna know what kind of freak you actually are!'

'It's freaky that you're so desperate to know the shape of my bits!'

'So you do *have* bits!' Gollum leered.

'It's not all about biology,' said Raven, head shaking in disbelief. 'Boy-girl. Girl-boy. It's not just what's in your pants; it's what's in your head that matters.'

'Well, I know what I got in my pants,' Jammo declared, thrusting his crotch in Raven's direction. 'I'm all big fat dick, me!'

'Yup – and you're a *dickhead* too,' said Raven with an angry grin. 'But I'm not judging – mate!'

CHAPTER 6
BUTTERFLIES

That evening, Kat opened the door to see Raven standing on her doorstep, grinning, in a plain white T-shirt, skinny jeans and Converse, hair up in a messy topknot. She felt her stomach lurch.

'Hi, project partner!'

Kat's mouth went dry and no words came out.

'So, if we're gonna do this homework thing, you're probably going to have to let me in.'

'Sure – yeah….' Kat stammered, blushing. Raven was just so…. Beautiful? Handsome? Sexy? It was hard to look away.

Kat led the way to her bedroom, then went to get drinks and snacks. When she came back she found Raven staring at the postcard collection over her desk – original cover designs for her favourite books.

'So I guess you really do love reading,' Raven said, glancing from a first edition cover of *The Great Gatsby* to another of *The Catcher in The Rye*.

'I guess,' Kat admitted, putting the tray down on the desk before she spilled stuff everywhere. Why was she so nervous? 'I figure when you're reading you climb into another person's head – or body – and walk around in it for a bit.'

'Body swapping – I like that idea,' said Raven.

Kat flipped open her laptop and they settled down on the floor to make a start on the project.

Raven was good at the visuals, fingers flying over the keyboard, finding images to match Kat's text. They were a good team and soon Kat forgot to be shy or nervous. The butterflies still lingered in her stomach – fluttering nervously every time her eyes met those sparkling blue ones. But it was so easy to be herself around Raven in a way that she had never really felt with anyone else.

'Are your parents – you know – supportive… you know about you being….'

'Gender-fluid?' Raven finished the sentence for her. 'Yeah – they've been great, you know… eventually. It took a bit of getting used to. For all of us. But we're getting there.'

'And school?'

Raven shrugged. 'The headmaster's been really great and the teachers… well, some are more open-minded than others.'

Kat nodded. 'I guess it's new for everyone.'

'Only it's not,' said Raven. 'Look at this book. Written a century ago. And there are gender-fluid stories dating back to Roman times.'

'I guess people don't like things they can't put a label on,' said Kat.

'Exactly! The one question everyone's gonna ask about our project is whether Orlando is a boy or a girl, right?'

'Because he starts out as a boy but by the end of the book she's a girl....'

'And says she/he's a bit of both!'

'Maybe everyone's a bit of both,' suggested Kat. 'Perhaps that's what the book is saying.'

'Maybe.' Raven's blue eyes were intent on hers now. She felt herself blushing. 'So what about you, Kat? You're a binary girl, right?'

'Binary?' Kat felt the blush deepen across her cheeks and down her throat as Raven's eyes continued to linger on her.

'All girl,' said Raven with a smile.

They were sitting side by side, backs against the bed, Raven's long, lithe legs laid out next to Kat's so they were just touching.

'You're also the most beautiful girl I've ever met, by the way.'

'And you're the most….' Kat couldn't finish the sentence.

Raven laughed. 'No need to fill in the gaps.' The laughing eyes met hers then strayed down to her lips and back again.

Kat found herself struggling to breathe properly as Raven's fingers brushed against her cheek, sending electrical currents through her skin.

'Is this OK?' Raven asked.

'Yes....' Kat felt as if she might crumple, dissolve.

Raven leaned towards her and their lips were millimetres apart.

Then she pulled away. 'I'm sorry – I....'

Raven sighed. 'No need to be sorry.' The words were spoken quietly, head turned away from hers.

'I just... I hardly know you,' she tried to explain.

'That's funny, because I feel like I've known you forever. Like I could talk to you about anything.'

'Me too,' said Kat. 'But....'

'But you need to know my "legal status"? If I'm a boy or a girl, right?'

'It doesn't matter to me, though.' Kat was surprised by her own words. 'That is – I know I fancy you either way.'

'Then why do you need to know?' Raven asked, looking at her straight in the eye now. 'I mean, legally, I have to tell you, cos if I don't this is classed as "assault". But why do you need to know so badly, I wonder?'

'For me,' Kat struggled to explain, 'I just need to know if I'm gay or straight, and how do I figure that out if I don't know whether I'm kissing a boy or a girl?'

'Maybe I'm both – and maybe so are you,' said Raven, a kind of urgent sadness in the blue eyes now. 'If I can live with that, why can't you?'

'I guess I'm not as brave as you are.'

'You care about what people might say about us?' said Raven. 'Is that it?'

'No, it's not about you,' Kat frantically tried to explain. Raven had turned away and she could feel the distance growing between them with every word she spoke. 'It's about me.'

‘Very original, Kat,’ Raven laughed bitterly, standing to leave. ‘I thought you were different. I thought you understood. Got me.’

‘I do. I get you,’ Kat scrambled to her feet, grabbing Raven’s sleeve. ‘I just don’t get me.’

Raven looked at her for a long moment then shook her hand away. ‘Well, when you figure yourself out, call me. Until then, I’m out, Kat.’

CHAPTER 7
EMPTY SEAT

In the form room the next day, Raven barely even looked in her direction. In girls' trousers with a boys' blazer and tie, hair pulled up in a loose ponytail and just a hint of lip gloss, Raven looked like a tall, beautiful young cadet. Sexy, remote and strangely sad.

'Do you want to work on the project together tonight?' Kat asked.

'I'm working in the school library,' Raven answered, eyes sliding off her and staring out of the window.

And Raven wasn't the only one who was icing her out. Somehow Saskia seemed to know about the homework 'date' at Kat's house. And she was not happy.

'I hear you and The Raven had an intimate homework session,' she said, deliberately putting her PE bag on the chair where Kat usually sat.

'We were doing the English project.'

'Right – that's what you're calling it these days,' Saskia laughed and turned away – without moving her bag.

Kat found an empty seat on the other side of the classroom and slumped down into it.

It was as if the mood in the class had shifted overnight. And it felt like everyone was talking about one thing. Jammo and his crew. The drama crowd. Even the geek squad in the corner was discussing the latest rumours.

'I heard Kat made a pass and The Raven knocked her back,' Saskia declared in a loud 'I-know-you-can-hear-me' whisper.

'Asexual,' Jammo was saying. 'That's what I heard. Nothing in the pants. No sex drive at all.'

'… I heard it was chopped off at birth cos it was so small they didn't know if it was a real dick….'

'… I read somewhere that they tuck it inside, make it into a fanny….'

'… I heard she/he's got both. You know – boy *and* girl bits stuffed in that G-string….'

'Does that mean it can have sex with itself?' Gollum guffawed.

'Like anyone else would want to….' said Saskia, with a giggle.

*

Throughout the next lesson – biology – Kat struggled to concentrate. Was it always like this for Raven at every new school? People were curious at first, until the novelty wore off and the puzzle remained unsolved, and then they grew hostile. Or was this the first time Raven had done it? A new start – a chance to break away from a boy/girl label? Was Raven even a real name? His/her real name?

Kat stared at the back of Raven's head across the biology lab. She kept recalling details from last night. Their legs touching, their faces so close, their lips millimetres apart. 'I hardly know you,' she had said. So why couldn't she get Raven out of her mind?

'Kat Collins, are you even listening?' She was broken out of her dream by Mr Brown, the biology teacher, who was staring at her – along with the rest of the class. The only person who wasn't looking at her was Raven.

'I'm sorry, sir. I was….'

'Staring into space?' suggested Mr Brown, sarcastically.

'Is that what you call it?' Jammo laughed. 'Just a face and a "space" where its bits should be.'

Raven didn't bother to turn around.

'Mr Jameson!' Mr Brown protested. 'We are supposed to be learning about asexual reproduction in plants.'

'Yeah – so how does that work again, sir?' asked Gollum. 'Is it like the tree has sex with itself?'

'And does it have both bits or no bits?' said Jammo.

'Is it just plants that do it, sir?' asked Saskia, shooting a look at Raven. 'Or can people do asexual stuff too?'

'Asexual reproduction in animals does occur,' said Mr Brown, who seemed unaware that a whole different conversation was actually going on here. 'In sea anemones and starfish, for example.'

'So Raven is a vegetable,' snorted Gollum.

'Or a jelly-creature from the deep,' giggled Saskia.

'The question is...' Jammo shot a glance at Raven's back, 'how do we figure out which?'

CHAPTER 8
LOSER

Lunchtime was more of the same. Muttering in the dining hall, comments and rumours flying down the corridors – everybody was talking about Raven.

Things came to a head on the sports field. They were doing sprint practice for sports day and one of the teachers was away, so they were all lumped together, boys and girls.

Kat – who hated running – didn't bother to listen to all the stuff Miss Powell was saying about sprint starts and dipping over the line. Everyone knew who would win anyway: Saskia was the fastest girl in the year and Jammo was the fastest boy. They'd come first in every race since Year 7. It occurred to Kat that this was probably why they ruled the school – in their different ways. Maybe it had always been like that since Stone Age times: the fastest/strongest man or woman becomes the natural leader.

Only where did that leave someone like Raven?

'Um – Miss – excuse me – but how is that fair?' Saskia protested when Raven stepped up to the starting line of the girls' race. 'I don't want to run against a...' she stopped, flailing for a word, 'a trannie!'

'Raven is not a transvestite,' said Miss Powell, rolling her eyes.

'Or transgender,' Raven added helpfully.

'And Raven has discussed this with me,' Miss Powell insisted.

'Come on, Sass, what you frightened of?' Gollum leered from the sidelines.

'Yeah? Don't you think you can beat it?' Jammo added.

'Of course I can.' Saskia flicked her ponytail. 'But that's not the point!'

Only it turned out, she couldn't. Raven, crouching on the starting line, looked like a statue of a young athlete, cast in marble, but when the gun fired it was like watching moving water. Raven's limbs seemed to flow through the buzzing heat, and Saskia didn't stand a chance as Raven sailed over the finish line several metres ahead of her.

It also turned out she was not a good loser.

'It's totally unfair! Why can't Raven do the boys' race?'

'I'm going to,' said Raven, breathless but grinning and triumphant.

Jammo, who had been wetting himself laughing about Saskia's defeat, stopped abruptly. 'Whoa! No way! I'm not racing against some ladyboy!'

'Why? Frightened you're gonna lose?' said Saskia, throwing his words back at him.

'I can beat the freak ten times over,' said Jammo, 'but Arthur/Martha can't race twice! What about the rules?'

'Funny – school rules don't usually bother you, Mr Jameson,' said Miss Powell. 'And Raven is not breaking any that I'm aware of.'

'Fine!' Jammo declared. 'Let's find out what the mutant can do against a real man!'

As Raven lined up at the start, Kat had a bad feeling in the pit of her stomach. It wasn't about the race any more. A bigger contest was going on here – and Raven couldn't win, no matter what happened.

The race started well – or at least Kat thought so because Raven stumbled at the start (due largely to a shove by Jammo) and by 50m Jammo was well in the lead.

But then something seemed to happen. It looked as if everyone else went into slow motion, with only Raven moving in normal time. The others seemed to fall back and, by 75m, Jammo was still in the lead but Raven was just behind and making up ground every second.

Kat saw Jammo glance anxiously over his shoulder. She watched Raven's long limbs moving like mercury, saw the set look of concentration in the intense blue eyes. She had said she hardly knew Raven but suddenly she realised she did. Because she knew that winning this race was about proving a point for Raven – no matter what it cost in the end.

Just 5m from the line they were neck and neck, but Jammo seemed to be tiring. Raven put on a final spurt of energy, surging ahead in the final few metres then dipping over the line in the dying seconds of the race to the shouts and screams of the rest of the class.

Kat thought Jammo would go mad but he didn't. He and Raven were both bent double, breathless, red-faced. Kat thought she saw Jammo turn and say something, but she couldn't make out what. Then he stood up and patted Raven on the back, grinning.

'Great run…' Miss Powell nearly added 'boys' but stopped herself just in time and said, 'kids.' 'Looks like we have a new champion to beat.'

'Beating sounds good,' muttered Jammo as the rest of the class clustered around Raven, back-clapping and congratulating. 'And this race ain't over yet.'

CHAPTER 9
THE RAVEN QUESTIONS

Kat couldn't concentrate on homework that night. She sat staring at the postcards above her desk, remembering the way Raven's long, slender fingers had trailed over them, the way those same fingers had lingered on her face.

Giving up on German verbs, she flicked on her computer and opened Facebook. To her surprise, Saskia had tagged her in a post. The comment just read: 'Ask Kat.'

With a sick feeling in her stomach, Kat clicked open the thread. It was from a new Facebook page called 'The Raven Question?'

'Boy or girl? Half and half? Or total mutant? You decide,' the description read. And there were photos of Raven, cleverly Photoshopped into a variety of poses and costumes. Raven as a princess, in a cheerleader's outfit, as a male stripper and a page three model.

There was a whole thread dedicated to Raven's pants and what might be in them. That's where Saskia had posted 'Ask Kat.' And her comment already had several replies.

'Has Kat been cravin' some Raven?'

'Kat and Raven – the mute and the mutant – getting it on?'

'Has The Kat been getting The Raven's cream?'

Kat couldn't read any more. She was about to click off the page when she spotted a new post, uploaded a few seconds ago. It was a livestream video entitled 'Savin' The Raven'. Sick with curiosity and fear, she opened it. Jammo's leering face appeared on the screen.

'Welcome to our live broadcast,' Jammo was saying 'Tonight we are on a mission to find the truth and save a confused kid from living a lie. Don't worry, Raven, the truth will set you free and this won't hurt – much!'

Kat's tried to take in what he was saying. The camera was panning round now and Kat could see that Jammo and his gang were down by the parade of shops near school. She glanced at her watch. It was nearly six. The school library would just be closing. Raven would be walking down the road any time now, past the shops, past Jammo and his gang.

'Stay tuned for a *big* revelation, folks!' Jammo was saying, camera in his face again.

'Or not so big!' snickered Gollum.

Kat scrambled in her pocket for her phone, her fingers fumbling as she tried to find Raven's number. She had to stop this happening.

But the mobile must have been turned off – library rules – and it went straight to answerphone.

'Raven!' she almost yelled at the voicemail. 'Jammo and his gang – they want to get you! Please – be careful!'

She hung up and rang again – and again – but it kept going to answerphone every time.

The livestream was still rolling on her laptop screen. She could see the shops, the road, with the school gates just out of sight. Then a voice behind the camera was yelling 'Buckle up, folks! Here comes The Raven!' And then she could see a tall familiar figure, about 100m away, walking right into the trap. She wanted to yell at the camera, yell at Raven to run, turn around and run!

She reached for her phone again. Maybe a text would work. Her fingers felt numb as they flew over the keyboard: 'Raven. It's a trap. Come to my house. Kat.' She pressed send and turned back to the screen. The figure of Raven was much closer now, close enough for her to see a hand reach into a pocket – for a text alert? But Raven kept walking....

The next bit happened so fast she could barely take it in. Jammo's face up close to the screen declaring, 'Operation Pant Patrol is go!' Then running figures, the camera wobbling, a flurry of bodies jumping Raven. Fists flying, the sounds of yells, thuds, an image of the sky then someone's foot, the scuffling of limbs, shouts, fists on flesh, flesh hitting tarmac, camera swinging drunkenly. And in the middle of it all, Raven – helpless, pinned down, dragged.

'Let's see what's in the trouser department....' Jammo was saying. Kat knew exactly what was going to happen next.

'Ready to zoom in!' Gollum yelled. 'Don't think we'll need a wide-angle lens for this shot!'

Kat turned away, unable to watch any longer.

She felt sick, angry, horrified. This went against everything Raven cared about, everything that mattered to the new kid who had fought so hard for personal privacy. And there was nothing she could do to stop it.

She snapped the lid shut and felt the tears begin to flow.

CHAPTER 10

NUMB

That was Friday night. By Sunday afternoon, Kat still hadn't heard anything. She was torn between a desperate need to know if Raven was OK and a determination not to go on social media to find out. She had to respect Raven's privacy. She owed Raven that much.

But there had been no response to any of her texts or messages. Saskia had tried to call a couple of times but Kat had blocked her. And as the time ticked on she couldn't stand not knowing any longer. She put on some lip gloss and mascara, and combed through her tangled brown hair.

'Mum, Dad, I'm just going out.'

'Where to?'

'To see a new friend.'

Her mum looked surprised but not unhappy. Her dad looked up from his paper. 'A girl-friend or a boy?'

'It's just Raven,' she answered with a shrug and a smile.

'Fine.' Dad returned his attention to the sports section. 'Just don't be back late.'

Ten minutes later, Kat was standing outside Raven's house in the pouring rain, her hair a sodden mess and her carefully applied make-up running down her face.

Raven opened the door wearing just a dressing gown.

'Hi.' Kat tried not to show how shocked she was at the sight of the black eye, the cut lip and the bruises visible through the open neck of the dressing gown.

'What are you doing here?' said Raven, not meeting her eye.

'I… we haven't finished the project,' said Kat, realising suddenly how pathetic that sounded.

'Not my problem,' said Raven. All the sparkle was missing from the beautiful blue eyes, which seemed dead and numb. 'I won't be coming back to school.'

'Until when?'

'Ever,' said Raven with a note of finality. 'My parents already applied to another school. We're moving again.'

'I don't understand….'

'Seriously?' Raven laughed bitterly. 'Are you telling me you are the only kid in the school who hasn't seen Jammo's video?'

'Actually, yes,' said Kat.

Raven's jaw tightened and the next few words sounded choked. 'You didn't watch it? Why?'

'I didn't need to know,' said Kat.

Raven laughed again, but this time it sounded almost like a sob of pain. 'Yeah – well, it's not like you won't find out everything the minute you walk into registration tomorrow.'

'I know,' said Kat quietly. 'That's why I needed to see you tonight.'

She was incredibly conscious that Raven was nearly naked under the dressing gown, and that bothered her more than she thought it would.

'I don't get you.' Raven's eyes met hers and Kat could hardly bear to think what Jammo and his mates had done to cause such an expression of pain.

'And I don't get you either,' said Kat, trying to find words to make things better while knowing that words could never be enough. 'But I… I don't need to. I don't care.

'Well, I hope that makes you feel better about yourself,' said Raven sarcastically.

'This isn't about me,' said Kat, suddenly desperate. 'It's about what they did to you. Did you even report it to the police?'

'My parents want me to,' said Raven with a shake of the head, expression hollow. 'But I don't have the energy to fight with people like that my whole life.'

'You can't let them get away with what they did to you,' Kat insisted. 'It was assault.'

'Yeah – I know. I was there – remember?'

Then Kat did something. Maybe it was the worst idea ever and Raven would hate her for it. But she had to do something and it was the only thing she could think of to do.

She moved forward and took step into the doorway. They were side by side now. Raven didn't move but looked tense, ready to spring out of the way at the slightest touch. Kat reached out, her fingers meeting the bruised cheek.

'Is this OK?' she asked.

Raven held her gaze for a long, long second, and Kat could see fear in the damp eyes that held hers.

Then Raven nodded. 'Yes – it's OK.'

The kiss was awkward, clumsy at first – wet and dry, cold and hot, half in and half out of the doorway. But still, somehow it felt right – normal, natural. They were two people who were attracted to each other – very attracted in Kat's case. Anything else – gender, sexuality – those things were just words. Labels. Boxes.

And they didn't matter any more.

CHAPTER 11

OLD NEWS

It was two weeks before Raven felt able to return to school. The bruises had nearly gone and the school rumour mill had moved on to the next 'big topic'. Nobody was talking about Jammo and his gang being arrested and suspended from school – and they'd stopped gossiping about the new 'gender-neutral' toilet block. All anyone was talking about now was Saskia Hardcastle's boob job and whether Miss Powell was having an affair with Mr Brown.

But Kat still knew how hard it was for Raven to walk back into the classroom that Monday morning. They arrived late after she'd insisted on scrubbing off the carefully applied make-up before they left.

'Don't cover up the scars,' she said. 'Let people see what they've done.'

'Like they've seen everything else,' said Raven. There was a hard anger staining the blue eyes now, and Kat wondered if it would ever fade.

'You do realise that the contents of your underwear drawer is old news,' said Kat. 'All anyone cares about now is Saskia's implants.'

Raven gave a nervous laugh, then stopped suddenly outside the classroom door. 'I'm not sure I can go in.'

'So where are you going to go then?' said Kat. 'Are you going keep swapping schools every time you come across a bunch of ignorant idiots?'

'I don't know,' said Raven. The bruises had faded but deep patterns of pain were still etched on the pale face.

'Cos that way you'll be, like, 97 before you take your GCSEs!' said Kat, reaching out to take Raven's hand in hers. It was cold, larger than her own, and her fingers fitted easily into the clammy palm.

Then she swung open the classroom door and watched Raven's expression change. Kat might not have read any of the posts on the 'Raven' Facebook page, but she had posted a message of her own last night. And it seemed like everyone had read it.

Because the whole class had been on a gender-bending uniform swap. They were all dressed in mix-and-match boy/girl uniform combos: blazers with skirts; trousers with ponytails and lip gloss – every combination you could think of.

'What is going on here?'

Kat turned around to see Mr Moles standing behind her, a look of bemusement on his piggy, red face.

'Yeah, Kat,' said Raven, turning to confront her, fingers dropping away from hers. 'What exactly is going on?'

Kat wondered for a second if she had totally misjudged things. 'I just thought… I mean….' She looked around the classroom. 'We wanted to show you… that we get it, you know?'

Raven frowned, taking in the mishmash of uniforms. 'You realise it's not just about clothing, right?'

'Yeah, we get that….'

'I'm not sure you really do,' sighed Raven.

'OK, but we're trying,' said Kat, fingers reaching out, clasping the hand tightly again. 'Is that OK for now?'

Raven looked around at the bunch of mix-and-match classmates, then turned to meet Kat's anxious gaze. 'I suppose it's a start.'

ABOUT THE AUTHOR

Catherine Bruton is the author of several critically acclaimed novels for teens and young adults, and has been described as 'one of the finest teen writers of recent years' (*The Guardian*). Her debut novel *We Can be Heroes* was recently adapted into a film starring Alison Steadman and Phil Davies. Later titles include *Pop!* and the multi-award-nominated *I Predict a Riot*. Catherine lives in Bath with her husband and two children, and teaches English part-time at King Edward's School.